Mark Zuckerberg
and
Facebook

INTERNET BIOGRAPHIES™

Mark Zuckerberg
and
Facebook

SUSAN DOBINICK

ROSEN
PUBLISHING®

New York

Published in 2013 by The Rosen Publishing Group, Inc.
29 East 21st Street, New York, NY 10010

Copyright © 2013 by The Rosen Publishing Group, Inc.

First Edition

Library of Congress Cataloging-in-Publication Data

Dobinick, Susan.
Mark Zuckerberg and Facebook/Susan Dobinick.
    p. cm.—(Internet biographies)
Includes bibliographical references and index.
ISBN 978-1-4488-6909-1 (lib. bdg.)
1. Zuckerberg, Mark, 1984– 2. Facebook (Firm) 3. Facebook
(Electronic resource) 4. Webmasters—United States—Biography.
5. Businesspeople—United States—Biography. 6. Online social
networks. I. Title.
HM479.Z83D63 2013
006.7092—dc23
[B]
                                                    2011045404

Manufactured in the United States of America

CPSIA Compliance Information: Batch #S12YA: For further information, contact Rosen Publishing, New York, New York, at 1-800-237-9932.

Contents

INTRODUCTION

From revolutionizing social interactions to spreading the word about social revolutions, Facebook has truly changed the world. It started as a pet project of Harvard University student Mark Zuckerberg, who was looking for a new and easy electronic way to browse his college's book that listed students with their photos. It has grown to become the second-most-visited site on the Internet (Google is the first), with an audience that now spans from college students to protesters to corporate executives. This is the story of how Facebook evolved from a Web site where college students connected with friends and flirted with each other to one of the most powerful and wealthiest technology companies in the world.

Facebook began as a Web site for students who attended Harvard and other Ivy League universities. Users were sorted into networks that were composed of other students at the same school. At first, users could only link their profile with others in their same network, but soon, they were able to connect with—or "friend"—users at other colleges of the Ivy League. Bit by bit, the Web site opened to students from other colleges, then high school students

and adults associated with specific work networks, and then, finally, to everyone age thirteen and older.

The site's growth in its early days was astonishing—and, as investors noted, extremely reliable. As soon as

For Mark Zuckerberg, founder and CEO of Facebook, one of the main purposes of the Web site is to figure out the many ways in which different people can connect with one other.

Facebook became available at a college, students signed up en masse. When it spread to teens and adults, some were skeptical that the company could make its mark beyond the college market. But now, years after the switch, Zuckerberg and his Facebook team have proven that people of all ages are interested in connecting with each other—and with different purposes as well. Many people still maintain personal profiles for meeting and communicating with friends. But now, companies also regularly update their business pages and launch social media campaigns that target prospective customers based on profile information. Activists use Facebook to meet like-minded individuals and to plan protests or spread news about injustices. Candidates for political office reach out to their supporters, soliciting donations and spreading information about their and their opponents' viewpoints. Journalists link to their most recent articles, and authors announce their upcoming books on their pages.

As the Web site opened to more people, it added more functions. People could interact with others on deeper levels, not just by adding them to lists of friends and sending messages, but also by sharing photos and other media and communicating in real time. Some of these innovations have led to creations that are focused on pure fun, such as popular games. Others have a greater purpose; the Facebook timeline feature aspires to tell the story of each user's life by listing relevant profile updates. Users select how much information to provide to viewers of their profile. In choosing how fully to fill out profiles and which extra features to include, users have the ability to create online identities. Because of Facebook's emphasis on users connecting with people whom they already know—unlike other social media Web sites like MySpace or Twitter—users, for the most part, aren't using these profiles to create new or fictitious online identities. Instead, they are extending their offline lives into these online worlds.

Filling out profiles allows young people especially to define themselves and show the world the way they see themselves. Through listing their favorite music and television shows, selecting groups to join and fan pages to support, and choosing their profile pictures, teens can clearly articulate to others the person that they see themselves becoming. Their public interactions—such as posting on each other's walls, liking status updates, or playing a game on the Web site together—make a statement about who they spend time with or with whom they are good friends. Hanging out after school has taken a new form because of Facebook. It's not just about going to the mall or the movies with friends; it's about interacting with each other online as well.

But sometimes, these Facebook interactions can take a nasty turn, resulting in everything from innocent misunderstandings that result in hurt feelings to deliberate cyberbullying that excludes or harms others. Profiles have become more complex and can offer fuller pictures of who people are, but the Web site itself offers plenty of opportunities for others to take advantage of the available information and the large and ready audience. Another concern is how easily college admissions staff and school officials can see teens' profiles, photographs, and other information posted about them. Teens may act differently around their friends than they do around authority figures. But if they do not select the proper privacy settings for their profiles, this information is accessible to everyone.

Outside of individual users' actions, Facebook has been the subject of much controversy, too. It has been repeatedly criticized for violating users' privacy and sharing or collecting information without their permission. Some say it is just a tool that gives advertisers too much information about consumers. And some wonder if Facebook was even Zuckerberg's idea to begin with: did he take advantage of the people who helped him the most during the early days? These controversies have led to public relations disasters at best, and lawsuits that have spanned years at worst. In addition to traditional media reporting on Facebook's actions, the site's users hold it accountable for its actions as well. Whether through commenting in status messages and on official blog posts or joining protest groups, users pay attention to—and make their opinions known about—each change the Web site makes.

Despite the accused missteps and misgivings that many have about the service, its reach is enormous. Facebook lists more than eight hundred million active users. That means more than eight hundred million people have signed onto the Web site within a given thirty days. Of those active users, Facebook estimates that more than 50 percent log in on any given day. Zuckerberg and his Facebook colleagues describe the way that people use the site as falling into something that they call the "Facebook trance." Users spend hours clicking from one person's profile to the next, going from one group page to another, with no particular end result in sight. They just want to see where the site will lead them next.

Zuckerberg, too, is curious as to what's next. Since its earliest days, Facebook has been a sought-after company. Zuckerberg has had many opportunities to sell the company. Each time, he has declined. He has turned down millions, and then billions, of dollars. He insists that, for him, Facebook is not about the money—he already has more than he will ever be able to spend. It's about figuring out how people live their lives online. It's about connecting the world in new and unexpected ways. And it's about seeing just how big his company can get.

CHAPTER 1

Before Facebook

Even as a child, Mark Zuckerberg was surrounded by technology, computers, and computer talk. He was born in 1984 in Dobbs Ferry, New York, a suburb north of New York City, to a dentist father and a psychiatrist mother. Although his father worked as a dentist, he was very interested in technology. So even though computers were not yet common in every household, Mark and his three siblings each had their own.

One of these early computers was an Atari 800. This computer was designed to look like a typewriter because its creators hoped it would be inviting to new users who were reluctant about new technology. Users inserted cassette tapes to access different programs. Most of these programs were games or typing lessons. One of the Zuckerberg family's computers included a program coding tape as well. Mark's father eagerly learned the basics from this tape. Soon after, he taught Mark what he had

The Atari 800 didn't have all of the functionality of modern computers, but it was the machine on which Zuckerberg first learned computer coding.

learned, and so began Mark's love of—and later, obsession with—computers.

After this early exposure to technology, Mark began to experiment in other ways with computers. His parents noticed his talent. They got him a personal tutor and later enrolled him in a graduate-level coding class. Mark built his first Web site in middle school using Geocities. Geocities was a free service that gave everyone with Internet access the tools to easily make their own personal Web sites. For many people Mark's age, Geocities Web sites were a way of

Young Adults and Facebook

For young adults, Facebook offers a specific set of possibilities and concerns. It is a new way of hanging out online. Young people can create profiles that describe how they see themselves to the world. They can communicate with friends. And they can even learn more about romantic prospects just by viewing their profiles. But it also means that young people can spread rumors, send photographs without permission, and tease each other much more easily. This behavior is known as cyberbullying. With cyberbullying, it is hard to control how quickly information spreads. A person can post a photograph or information that will reach many people at once. Even if the original poster removes it, other users may have already seen, saved, or passed along the information. Some schools have specific rules against cyberbullying, even if it is done outside of school hours. On local, state, and national levels, politicians are considering laws that make cyberbullying a crime.

creating a personal identity online. Some Web sites were dedicated to favorite television shows or celebrities, but some were profilelike lists of users' favorite things. This was one of the first times that people realized how easy it was to create and share their own content online.

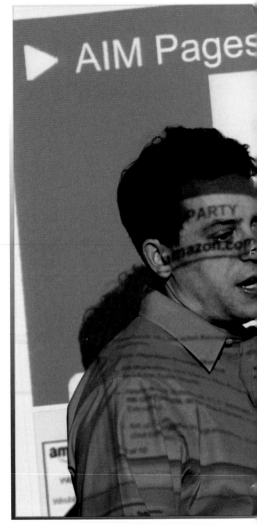

As Mark grew older, his computer experiments became more complicated. He created a computer version of the game Risk. He invented a system to message his siblings on their computers, using the same technology that the creators of AOL Instant Messenger (AIM) would later use. When AIM did become popular, Mark created a program that let him know when other users changed their away messages. (Away messages were short, often witty messages that people wrote to say what they were doing when they stepped away from their computers.) He would later use these messages as inspiration for the status update feature on Facebook.

In school, Mark was a multitalented but discontented student. He transferred to a private school called Phillips

James Bankoff was AOL's executive vice president for programming and products. AOL Instant Messenger showed people a new way of connecting instantly online, and it also inspired some of Facebook's features.

Exeter Academy after he complained that his two years at Dobb Ferry's public high school were boring. At his new private school, he fenced, studied ancient foreign languages, and received awards for his skills in physics, astronomy, and math. Of course, he continued to work with computers.

As a senior project, he and a classmate, Adam D'Angelo, created a program called Synapse. Synapse predicted a user's musical taste based on his or her listening habits. Mark and Adam posted the program online for free. Companies including Microsoft and AOL were impressed and offered up to $1 million to buy the program. Mark and his classmate declined at first. Then after they began college, they reconsidered the offer and returned to the companies. But it was too late—the tech companies were no longer interested.

THE HARVARD EXPERIMENTS

While still a freshman at Harvard University, Zuckerberg was known around campus as a computer whiz. There were even rumors that he was on an FBI watch list for his hacking skills. Despite being well known, though, Zuckerberg was often viewed as shy and awkward, so he wasn't very popular. Still, he made friends with other students who were interested in computers, and he pledged a Jewish fraternity, Alpha Epsilon Pi.

A young Mark Zuckerberg programs on campus at Harvard in 2004, several months after he had established and become known for Thefacebook. In many ways, he was just a typical college student.

The summer after his freshman year, Zuckerberg worked at a programming job that paid well, but he found it boring and unrewarding. He preferred to spend his time with Adam D'Angelo, his friend who had helped him create

Harvard's Kirkland House dorm was where Zuckerberg lived during his sophomore year. It was also the home of Facebook during its earliest days.

Synapse. D'Angelo had also had some success with another program he created, called BuddyZoo. It was a supplement to the AIM program, and it allowed users to compare their buddy lists—lists of users they communicated with. Zuck-

erberg and D'Angelo spent hours contemplating what the future of the Internet could be, especially how people would communicate online. AIM had been a large part of teenage lives for many people their age. Would it stay on top? Or would something new come along to topple it?

At the start of Zuckerberg's sophomore year at Harvard, he moved into a tiny suite dorm with three young men he did not yet know. The room quickly became a mess of clothes and empty bottles, piles of papers and computer wires. One of the roommate's girlfriends became certain that the only time their common room was clean was when she picked it up for them.

Zuckerberg was preparing for the new school year and new courses, but inspired by his summertime conversations,

The Origin of "Facebook"

Facebooks were common at colleges, and even at some high schools, across the country. At the start of freshman year, schools' administrators would distribute a printed booklet that listed the name and included a picture—the identification card photograph—of each student in the class. For all four years of undergraduate education, students would use these books as a resource to identify classmates. Harvard University students could access electronic versions of these facebooks only for students who lived in their dorms. At the time that Mark created Facemash, students at Harvard and other colleges and universities were begging administrators to create complete electronic versions of their facebooks.

he was also pondering the social future of the Internet. He didn't wait long to create his own part in it.

Zuckerberg used his classmates' usernames and passwords. He broke the rules to connect to the Internet in other dorms. He hacked into campus Web sites. Through these means, he managed to download nine "facebooks" that were typically accessible only to students who lived in those dorms. He then loaded them all onto one Web site. Two students' pictures would appear at a time on the screen, and the user was asked to vote on which person was more attractive. The text on the screen seemed to make Zuckerberg's intentions behind the Web site clear: "Were we let into Harvard for our looks? No. Will we be judged for them? Yes."

The journal posted along with the program said that Zuckerberg completed the program in an eight-hour, beer-fueled stretch. He posted the Web site, Facemash, the following afternoon and sent the link to a few friends, who sent it on to a few more. By that evening, hundreds of visitors had voted on thousands of pairs of photographs. Some students who used the program found it addicting, but some student organizations complained of sexism and racism. Harvard's computer service department shut down the program, but not before Zuckerberg's computer crashed because of the Web site's heavy traffic.

Zuckerberg and the two other students who assisted him were sent to the school's disciplinary board. His friends were released, but the board charged him with violating the school's security, copyright, and privacy codes. The board ordered him to seek counseling and warned that he would remain on probation. Zuckerberg apologized to the offended student groups, saying that he saw the Web site just as a computer project—he didn't mean for it to become so public. To make up for it, he agreed to set up a Web site for one of the groups. He celebrated his light punishment soon after by sharing an expensive bottle of champagne with his hall mates.

Harvard's student newspaper carefully followed the Facemash incident through articles and editorials, so any student who hadn't experienced the Web site firsthand could read about it. One editorial in particular noted that Facemash wouldn't have gotten Zuckerberg into so much trouble if he had just given students the option of using the program instead of including students without their consent. Another scolded the college's administration, saying that if a student could create Facemash, then the school certainly had the ability to create a facebook for the whole college. Zuckerberg has said that these editorials, as well as a detailed conversation with computer science classmates, inspired him and helped him to figure out how Facebook should be set up. But not everyone believes that Zuckerberg's ideas came about so innocently.

His later successes were often credited to his ability to understand what people wanted. When his fellow students were deciding which classes to take, they didn't always think in terms of academics. They wondered which classes their friends would be in. So the first week of school, Zuckerberg created a program called Course Match. The program showed which students were signed up for which classes. Course Match offered an easy way for students to figure out how their course load might affect their social lives. Were cool students in their classes? Which classes could they take to spend more time with the people they were interested in? Course Match became addictive and spread through the campus in no time.

Soon after, Zuckerberg applied his computer skills to his controversial project, the program called Facemash. According to a journal that he posted along with the program, he was upset after an argument that he had with a woman. He was looking for a distraction. First he thought about making a program that compared students to animals, asking users to rate who was more attractive. A friend said that perhaps it would be better to mostly compare classmates to each other and only occasionally

The movie *The Social Network* dramatized the founding of Facebook, telling a story filled with partying and betrayal. Company insiders say the film greatly exaggerated many aspects of the real story.

include animals. Even though the final version did not include animals at all, Zuckerberg's open commentary caused the program to become the target of criticism, both at the time it was created and years later, when the story was exaggerated in *The Social Network*, the 2010 feature film about the birth of Facebook.

CREATOR OR COMPETITOR?

Of course, Zuckerberg wasn't the only student at Harvard who worked on projects. The university is teeming with ambitious students. One particular society on campus looked for members whom it believed would be the future business leaders of the world, with students joking that if its alumni didn't make their first million by the age of thirty, the club would give it to them.

It was in this environment that twin brothers Tyler and Cameron Winklevoss and their friend Divya Narendra had been working on a Web site idea they called HarvardConnection. The three weren't programmers, but they thought they could change how people dated at Harvard. Their Web site would initially be open to Harvard students only. Later, they hoped it would slowly spread to other colleges across the country. The Web site would compile lists of local nightclub events and maybe

The *Harvard Crimson* reported the controversy over Facemash and steadily followed Zuckerberg's successes, as well as setbacks and controversies, with Facebook.

even suggest who students might be interested in dating. Users would create profiles, connect with friends, and send messages to each other using the Web site.

Two former classmates of the Winklevosses and Narendra had started to set up the Web site, but both had left

Twins Cameron and Tyler Winklevoss were Zuckerberg's classmates at Harvard. They claim that he stole their idea for a social networking Web site, which eventually became Facebook.

the project before completing it. When the Winklevosses and Narendra read about Facemash in the Harvard newspaper, they were convinced that Mark Zuckerberg was the person who could help them launch their Web site. They met with him, and he agreed to help them with it. They provided him with the passwords to access the work that had already been completed, and Zuckerberg assured them that HarvardConnection would be up and running soon.

THE DISAGREEMENT

What happened next isn't clear. The Winklevosses and Narendra both e-mailed and called Zuckerberg regularly to check in, and his responses varied. Yes, the Web site was going fine, he told them, but he was swamped with class work and couldn't work on the site as often as he had hoped. They met once in his dorm room, and on a dry erase board, they saw a few lines of computer code written under the words "Harvard Connection." They were anxious to launch but couldn't do it without Zuckerberg's help. They were hopeful that he would be done soon. Thanksgiving and then winter break rolled by, and they still didn't have any word about when HarvardConnection would be complete. Zuckerberg met with the HarvardConnection team as late as three days after he had already registered the domain name for Thefacebook.com. The team said he told them that their work would be done soon. He never mentioned his work on his own Web site.

Thefacebook launched on February 4, 2004, and the team behind HarvardConnection read about it in their college newspaper two days later. Zuckerberg insisted he had done nothing wrong—all social networking sites borrowed from the same ideas. He often used the argument that a person who had invented one chair could not sue a person who invented another chair. He pointed to HarvardConnection's focus on dating as a major difference. The Winklevosses and Narendra pointed to the profile setup and college exclusivity as evidence that Zuckerberg had stolen their idea and taken code intended for the HarvardConnection site to create his own. HarvardConnection was renamed ConnectU and launched later that spring, but it never reached as large an audience as they had hoped. As they had discussed with Zuckerberg, the key to success online was being the first Web site of its type, and Thefacebook had beaten them to it.

CHAPTER 2

The Launch

Whether HarvardConnection's claims against Facebook were valid, it's true that the site Mark Zuckerberg created borrowed elements of many different social networks from the time. Friendster was a popular social network that allowed people to see profiles and lists of their friends' friends. It was based on the idea that you might be connected through a friend to someone you'd like to date. MySpace, a network that allowed people to create profiles using any username and encouraged meeting new people on the Internet, was taking off, too. In later years, a program called FriendFeed, created by former Google employees, would inspire new Facebook features until Facebook finally bought out the company.

Zuckerberg wasn't the first person to create a college-specific social networking Web site. In 2001, a student at Stanford University created a multipurpose social network called Club Nexus. Around the time that Zuckerberg

Plug-in FAQ

[thefacebook]

home   search   global   social net   invite   faq   logout

[My Friends]

[export]

nds

[global]

Export contact information f
in Outlook and other progr

[invite]

Find friends at other schools.

nvite friends to join thefacebook.

[Other Schools]   [GWU]   [All]

Edit Friends

Filter: [Recently Updated Profiles]

You have 247 friends.

[message]   [remove]

KIP ABER
profile updated recently

[message]   [remo

Steph Adams

Adlakha

Early on, Thefacebook.com allowed users to connect with only friends at colleges and universities. The Web site's functions were limited compared with Facebook today.

was working on Facebook, Columbia University and Yale University had developed their own online communities. Even at Harvard, a student named Adam Greenspan created a Web site in 2003 called houseSYSTEM, which listed class reviews and served as a marketplace for used books. It also allowed users to include a photograph of their own choice. (Greenspan later sued Zuckerberg and settled for an undisclosed amount).

So combining Harvard students' interest in an online version of their facebook and the tech world's interest in connecting people in new ways, Zuckerberg got to work. One of the first people he told about his idea was Eduardo Saverin, a fellow Harvard student who was known around campus for his hobby of investing. Zuckerberg knew that he would need start-up cash. He asked Saverin to invest $1,000 in exchange for a one-third interest in the company, and he invested $1,000 of his own money as well. Zuckerberg spent all winter break coding and creating what his friends thought was just another of his many projects. When students returned to classes, he launched the Web site.

INITIAL RECEPTION

Thefacebook spread quickly. Zuckerberg sent it first to a couple of friends and then to the e-mail list of his entire dorm. They sent it to their friends, and by the end of February, about three-quarters of the student population at

The Saverin Lawsuit

Eduardo Saverin's return to Harvard was the end of his involvement as an employee of Thefacebook. The company would later sue him for blocking access to bank accounts during this time and because he claimed that he was still entitled to a 30 percent stake in the company. Saverin countersued, saying that he was entitled to these shares because of his early investments in, and work for, the company. Their deal was eventually settled out of court. Saverin received an undisclosed percentage of the company and his name was added to the cofounders list on the company's Web site.

Harvard had signed up. Some staff, faculty, and alumni were also able to sign up because they, too, had Harvard e-mail addresses.

The Web site's functions were limited and simple. Users uploaded a photo of their own choosing. Unlike the ID card photographs that Mark had uploaded for Facemash, these pictures were flattering. Users filled out a profile listing contact information, interests, current classes, and relationship status. Once the profiles were complete, they could add friends. In Facebook's early days, and even for

Eduardo Saverin, a cofounder of Facebook, became well known for his lawsuit against Mark Zuckerberg.

some users today, part of the fun was seeing how many friends you could get. Users could press a button to "poke" other users. Poking had no real meaning—Facebook's frequently asked questions (FAQ) page told users that poking was a feature used just for fun—although many interpreted it as a way to flirt. And reminiscent of Course Match, users could see if any of their connections were in their classes. The Web site was filled only with information that each user chose to provide. Zuckerberg had learned from the earlier Facemash incident that respecting users' privacy was key to establishing a long-lasting Web site—and to staying out of trouble with the college's administration.

His intentions in creating Thefacebook were to give students the service they had been asking for from the administration for so long—but also to create a new way for people to connect to each other. He required that everyone who registered did so using a Harvard e-mail address. This allowed him not only to keep the network exclusive, but also to ensure that users really were who they claimed to be. His social networking Web site sought to connect people who already knew each other, unlike MySpace, which encouraged people to connect with new friends. But mainly, Zuckerberg said, Thefacebook was always about creating a more open world.

Thefacebook was so well received at Harvard that Zuckerberg started making plans to move the Web site beyond the university. But with its fast-spreading success, he needed help. After all, he wasn't just the creator of a Web site that students were crazy about. He was also still a college student with a full course load. So, as many college students might do when looking for help, he turned to his roommates. Dustin Moskovitz was one, and he quickly taught himself computer coding so that he could handle much of the day-to-day maintenance of the Web site. Chris Hughes was another of Zuckerberg's roommates, and he handled publicity and the growing number of interview requests. With the help of these two, and Eduardo Saverin's continued support on the business side, Thefacebook started to expand.

THE SPREAD

Zuckerberg was convinced that exclusivity was key to Thefacebook's success. So at first, he decided to restrict the site's membership to Ivy League and other top-rated schools. In this sense, just being able to have Thefacebook was a status symbol. The crew set up the Web site at other schools. Initially, they allowed users to only view profiles from students at their own school, but it soon became clear that users wanted to be able to connect with friends at other schools. They set up a system that allowed users to view profiles from students at these schools if both users agreed, forming the basis of the Facebook friendship that the Web site still uses today.

Sean Parker

Sean Parker is a well-known person in the tech world. When he was just out of high school, he helped create Napster, a program that allowed users to download music and other media from each other for free. Napster was one of several such file-sharing programs, but it was the most popular, so it received the most attention, good and bad. Record companies accused the program of knowingly allowing the illegal exchange of files. Parker lost his job in the middle of many lawsuits that faced the company.

He went on to cocreate another company called Plaxo, whose primary function was similar to an electronic address book. Plaxo was successful, but its venture capitalists, people who had invested a lot of money in exchange for shares in the company, doubted Parker's ability to be a successful leader. He had a reputation for partying too much, and he was not very strict about business deadlines or schedules. The investors had enough power to fire him, and he was left with no stake in, or money from, the company.

Now students from colleges outside the Ivy League wanted in, too. Zuckerberg received dozens of e-mails daily from interested people, wanting to know when their college would be added. The word was spreading across the country, and the founders couldn't keep up with the demand. Even adding the help of Adam D'Angelo, co-creator of the Synapse music program and creator of BuddyZoo, wasn't enough. By the end of the semester, Thefacebook had more than one hundred thousand users nationwide. Zuckerberg, Moskovitz, D'Angelo, and another computer programming classmate, Andrew McCollum, decided to rent a house in Palo Alto, California, the center of the tech world, and dedicate the summer to Thefacebook. Saverin would be working on Thefacebook in his own way, too. He had a summer internship in New York, but he would also be setting up meetings with possible advertisers. He also put another $10,000 of his own money into the company's bank account.

THE MOVE

Soon after their arrival in Palo Alto, the Thefacebook team met up with Sean Parker cocreator of Napster. Parker had contacted Zuckerberg months before when he first heard about Thefacebook. He traveled to meet Zuckerberg and Saverin at an expensive restaurant in New York. He overdrew his bank account to pay for the meal because he was inspired by the site's work. Parker thought that social networks would be the next big thing on the Internet, and he offered to introduce Zuckerberg to his connections in the tech world who thought the same. Zuckerberg respected Parker because Parker knew about the trials of start-up Internet companies very well. Zuckerberg also admired him because of his involvement in Napster, which was a popular program that, like Thefacebook, had a lot of young users. Parker happened to be moving out of his apartment, so it was quickly decided that he would move in with Thefacebook team. Not long after, Zuckerberg asked him to come on as the president of Thefacebook.

The house quickly took on an appearance similar to Zuckerberg and Moskovitz's old dorm room in Harvard's Kirkland House—they piled up trash in the midst of messes of computers and cords. Thefacebook wasn't a typical summer job, so the team didn't work nine-to-five hours. They slept as late as they wanted, then wandered downstairs in their pajamas and worked late into the night. Sometimes Zuckerberg would declare that the team was on lockdown, which meant they couldn't leave their computers until they had finished whatever they were working on.

Zuckerberg and D'Angelo spent a lot of time working on a service that they wanted to add to Thefacebook called Wirehog. Wirehog would give users access to, and the ability to download from, the files on their friends' computers. Parker cautioned Zuckerberg against this

As a cofounder of the music-sharing site Napster before working with Facebook, Sean Parker was known in the technology world for his bright ideas, ability to sniff out new trends, and partying lifestyle.

service. He knew from his days at Napster that sharing media files led to copyright concerns, and record and movie companies were eager to stop this sort of file sharing. He wondered if connecting Wirehog to Thefacebook could lead to lawsuits that would destroy the entire company. After months of debate, Zuckerberg eventually gave in to Parker and abandoned the project. But for that first summer, the idea of figuring out a way to allow this sharing took up much of the company's time. D'Angelo even told people that he worked for Wirehog, not Thefacebook.

When the group wasn't working, they threw parties, inviting local college students through advertisements on

Napster was one of the first peer-to-peer file-sharing programs. It allowed users to download music, videos, and pictures from each other for free, and often illegally.

Thefacebook. They installed a zip line over the pool, and Zuckerberg could often be found fencing in the backyard, shouting quotes from *The Aeneid*, an ancient epic poem about the Trojan War, while trying to think out a problem.

A PRESIDENT'S ROLE

In his new role of company president, Parker handled the many companies that courted Thefacebook. Some sought to outright buy it, while others wanted to invest in it. Zuckerberg was not prepared to sell Thefacebook. His interest wasn't in money, he said, but in seeing how big it could get and in changing the way that people interacted with each other.

Still, running Thefacebook was getting expensive. Its initial start-up costs were low, with just the monthly fee for use of the domain name. But as more users joined, Thefacebook had to buy servers that allowed the Web site to function properly with so much traffic. (Servers are computers that are dedicated to just running the function of a particular Web site.) Friendster's inability to handle its large number of users was the reason many people gave for its downfall. Zuckerberg was determined not to make the same mistake. So they opened to new universities only as they had the capability to, and Parker started to look more seriously into funding options.

He invited companies such as Google to Facebook's messy headquarters, and the team made no special efforts to clean up or act professionally to impress them. But they didn't have to—companies were still interested. So far that summer, Zuckerberg had spent tens of thousands of his own and his parents' money for servers and to pay salaries. Saverin was working on finding more investors in New York, but he was more and more disconnected from Parker's efforts to get larger funding in Palo Alto. Frustrated with the lack of communication, and with what he viewed as a slight, he froze the company's bank account.

Around this time, Parker helped Zuckerberg incorporate Thefacebook into an official corporation. They split the shares between Zuckerberg, Parker, Moskovitz, Saverin, and a law firm that helped them file the paperwork. The new agreement overrode all previous agreements that Zuckerberg had made, as well as some small steps that Saverin had taken earlier in an attempt to incorporate the company. In this new agreement, each individual's shares were subject to dilution, which meant that the person could become worth less money as the number of shares in the company increased. This agreement led to a later lawsuit, settled for an undisclosed amount, between Saverin and Zuckerberg. By the end of the summer, Saverin returned to Harvard. Zuckerberg and Moskovitz found a new house in Palo Alto and decided to put aside finishing college for now.

CHAPTER 3

Growing Pains

As fall arrived, Thefacebook had two hundred thousand users and was set to expand to dozens of colleges and universities as soon as the term began. But the people behind Thefacebook were still without access to the site's bank account. They were broke. Luckily, Sean Parker had found the perfect investor for them: Peter Thiel, who had cofounded PayPal, a company that allowed people to securely pay for goods and services online using their credit cards or bank account information. Thiel was not interested in controlling the company. He trusted Mark Zuckerberg and wanted to see where Thefacebook would go.

Zuckerberg and Parker believed this made Thiel the ideal business partner. He invested $500,000, which valued the company at $4.9 million. Thefacebook could continue on for a while, anyway, without worrying too much about money.

Peter Thiel is one of the most well-respected venture capitalists in the technology world. Sean Parker and Mark Zuckerberg thought he was the perfect person to provide financial backing to TheFacebook.

WALLS AND GROUPS

With money problems out of the way for now, Thefacebook celebrated the start of the new school year with some big changes to the Web site. Most notably, it featured the "wall." Each person's profile now featured a section where friends could write and view public comments. This added a new layer to the interactions on the Web site. Before, a user could be friends with someone, but with so many users competing to have as many friends as possible, it was hard to tell how well one person knew another. Now, when users left messages on each other's walls, they showed that they were friends on a deeper level. It wasn't just straightforward communication. It was also a way for users to learn more about each other and tell others more about themselves. This became a huge draw, leading users to spend even more time on the Web site.

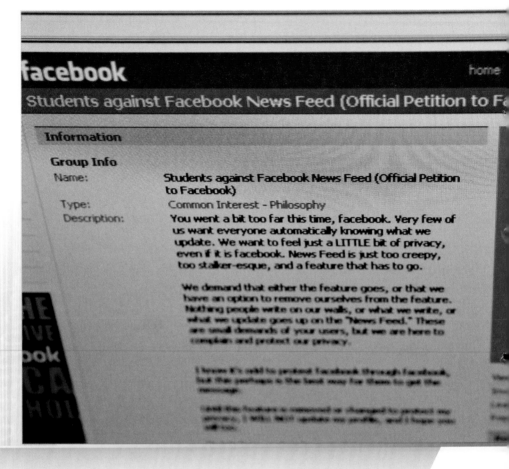

Users joined groups with many different purposes on Facebook. Sometimes, this included protesting changes to the site itself.

Another major change was the introduction of groups. People could join groups based on common interests, courses, or even inside jokes. In addition to allowing for new ways to interact, groups were also important to Thefacebook for one major business reason: companies could pay Thefacebook to create official groups and

advertise directly to possible consumers. The Web site covered its entire monthly costs just through a deal for an official group for Apple. This type of advertisement was appealing to Zuckerberg because he thought it was important that users' experiences on Thefacebook were always as easy and natural as possible. When Eduardo Saverin was still involved, he and Zuckerberg fought about including an extra click to add a friend, which would allow more time to show advertisements. Groups and flyers, which were ads that individual students or student groups could buy to target their own school, were the types of advertising that Zuckerberg felt didn't interrupt Thefacebook experience.

FINDING FUNDING

Still, as Thefacebook climbed up past one million users, it became more and more expensive to run. Zuckerberg had an awkward relationship with prospective investors. He knew that he would need their help, but he resented their involvement anyway. His behavior toward them at this time sometimes showed that, despite being in charge of the hottest company in Palo Alto, he was still just a twenty-year-old without much of an idea of how to run a business. As a snub to one investment firm with whom Parker had a bad history, Zuckerberg and Parker showed up late to a meeting. They were dressed in their pajamas, and they made a presentation listing the top ten reasons that company should not invest in them. The company got the point. It didn't make an offer. Years later, Zuckerberg said he regretted being so rude to them.

Still, Thefacebook could afford to turn down anyone it wanted. There were plenty of other companies that wanted in. Through the father of a classmate from Harvard, Zuckerberg was able to meet with executives at the *Washington Post* newspaper company. He was especially impressed by Donald Graham, the chief executive officer (CEO). He respected the work of journalists, and he knew that becoming involved with the *Washington Post* would be a different sort of partnership than becoming involved with venture capitalists would be. Venture capitalists would be concerned with making the company grow. Graham, who was dedicated to enhancing the *Post*'s Web presence, insisted that they would not interfere in this way. The *Post* was interested in looking at long-term goals, Graham assured Zuckerberg. There would be no pressure to make money and then sell Thefacebook quickly at a high profit.

Jim Breyer, a partner at Accel Partners, currently serves on Facebook's board.
He has played a large role in discussions on the future of the company.

Graham was impressed by the company. A Harvard graduate himself, he had worked for the school's daily student newspaper, the *Harvard Crimson*, during his college years, and he fondly remembered the notebook that he and his fellow staff members used to facilitate meetings. They left messages for each other about the newspaper as well as their own activities. Graham thought that Thefacebook tapped into the very same desire to communicate and connect that had made the notebooks so important to the newspaper staff. He saw Thefacebook as a way to make this sort of communication accessible to the online world.

With Zuckerberg and Graham equally dedicated to the match, the *Washington Post* offered to invest $6 million in exchange for 10 percent ownership of the company. Despite other companies' interest—including an offer from media giant Viacom to straight-out buy Thefacebook for $75 million and incorporate it into its subsidiary MTV.com—it seemed like the deal with the *Post* was about set.

Then Accel Partners, a venture capital firm with a lot of financial backing, approached. Its offer was too good to refuse. Accel would make a large investment that valued Thefacebook at $98 million.

Parker encouraged Zuckerberg to go forward with the deal, but Zuckerberg was reluctant. He felt that he had made a promise to Graham. At a dinner with Accel, he

ConnectU

The HarvardConnection team first tried to resolve the dispute by going to the president of the university. They claimed that Zuckerberg had broken the student code of conduct. The president declined to get involved, so the Winklevoss twins contacted an attorney and sent Zuckerberg a cease-and-desist letter just days after Thefacebook launched. Zuckerberg maintained that he had not stolen anyone's ideas, saying that when a person is successful, others often try to latch onto that success. When the letter did not have any effect on Thefacebook's operations, the HarvardConnection—by then, ConnectU—team took the issue to court. Facebook countersued, saying ConnectU was illegally collecting information from Facebook's Web site to solicit users for its Web site. The Winklevoss twins eventually settled out of court for an estimated $65 million in cash and stock. However, they later claimed that the stock part of their settlement was not valued as highly as Facebook had said and that it dropped the settlement's value to about $32 million. ConnectU filed an appeal but was denied in May 2011.

left the table and did not return. When one of his coworkers came to check on him, he was in the bathroom crying because he said he felt like he was facing a moral dilemma. Accel would give Thefacebook the money the site needed, but Zuckerberg admired Graham.

Finally, he called Graham to discuss the problem. He told him that he was sure that Accel Partners would just keep increasing its offer, and right now, money mattered for Thefacebook. Graham admired Zuckerberg's openness—he was sorry to not go forward with the deal, but he told Zuckerberg to do what he thought he had to do for the company.

Finally, Zuckerberg and Parker accepted Accel Partners' deal. As a plus, the company gave signing bonus money to Zuckerberg, Parker, and Moskovitz. So once again, Thefacebook would no longer have to worry about money for a little while. Now, for the first time, Zuckerberg, Parker, and Moskovitz were millionaires.

FINDING AN IDENTITY

With money in hand, Thefacebook's next step was to work on recruiting more employees. For the most part, the company was filled with young men in their early through mid-twenties. Zuckerberg wanted to keep what he saw as a cool and relaxed atmosphere at Thefacebook. So he looked down on many of the executives that recruiters tried to convince him to hire. He preferred to go to local schools like Stanford University and chase down the top computer students. When someone who seemed particularly talented interviewed for an internship, he might tell the person that the company was only hiring for full-time positions, forcing the person to choose between Thefacebook and school. Zuckerberg convinced some employees to leave Google, LinkedIn (a networking Web site dedicated to professionals), and other hot Web companies.

But the company's laid-back atmosphere didn't appeal to everyone. Some people refused to work there, saying that a company run by a well-known party boy (Parker) and a twenty-one-year-old who didn't know anything about business (Zuckerberg) was only headed for disaster. And some of Thefacebook's strategies on the business side were unusual at this early stage. One of the few women who worked there complained of sexual harassment. Zuckerberg's way of dealing with it was to make a joke about how ridiculous the harasser's word choice was at a company meeting.

Zuckerberg communicated with his employees via AIM, even if they were in the same room with him, which some employees found unsettling. One recruiter eventually realized that she had to stay up and take part in late-night instant-messaging chats because it was when all the big decisions were made.

Facebook's offices in the early days were known for their long hours of both working and partying.

In the office, the walls were decorated with graffiti. Conference rooms were equipped with video game systems and beach chairs. Thefacebook offered a housing allowance to employees who lived within walking distance. Many employees lived, and partied, together just a few blocks from the office.

The party culture would lead to the end of Parker's time at Thefacebook. He, his assistant, and some other friends rented a vacation house in the fall of 2005, and they threw several parties. The police raided the house and allegedly found cocaine, as well as the assistant, who was under the legal drinking age, drinking beer. Parker was never formally charged with a crime, but the investors at Accel Partners were upset. They were particularly disturbed that Parker had been caught with an underage employee. They demanded that he leave the company.

Zuckerberg was hesitant about this. Parker had served as an important mentor and sounding board. He once said that he didn't know which ideas were his and which were Parker's because they shared so much. Still, as Thefacebook was growing, it was becoming less about a group of friends doing something cool and more about Thefacebook becoming a business. Zuckerberg decided that Parker leaving might be for the best, and Parker agreed to step down.

Parker's departure didn't automatically make the company into a business, however. Zuckerberg still had plenty of learning of his own to do. He was used to being sought after by possible investors and buyers, and he was a naturally curious person. With Parker gone, he started to handle these interactions himself. He didn't wonder how much money the companies might give him if he sold Thefacebook—he wondered how these other companies worked. So he openly and regularly accepted meeting requests, trying to learn more about these companies. But employees didn't understand Zuckerberg's actions. Each time he met with top executives outside the company, rumors would swirl around Thefacebook offices. Was he trying to sell? Would everyone lose their jobs, or,

Profile pages on Facebook offer users several different ways to express themselves through pictures, groups, and lists of interests.

for the earlier workers who had stock options, become millionaires?

With the company on edge, a trusted colleague finally confronted Zuckerberg. "You'd better take CEO lessons," she told him, according to the book *The Facebook Effect*, written by David Kirkpatrick. Zuckerberg realized then that he had to change the way he thought of himself as a boss. He took classes on how to be an executive, shadowed his mentors, and finally, stopped accepting every meeting. He talked

Target exactly the audience

Location
Country
State
City or Town
Age
Gender
Interests
Activities
Music

Boo
TV
Edu
Hi
Co
Ma
Wo
Pol
Rel

As Mark Zuckerberg became more serious about building Facebook into a business, he realized the importance of focusing on goals and fostering positive public interest.

about goals and promised to try to communicate better, but mostly, he emphasized that he wasn't trying to get rid of the company. He still just wanted to see how big it could get.

A NEW NAME AND NEW FACES

Fall was becoming the traditional time for change at Thefacebook. Students returned to school, which increased site traffic. New students would become eligible for their own accounts. So in the fall of 2005, the company prepared to launch another school year with some major changes.

The first major change was one of the last reminders of Sean Parker's work at the company: Thefacebook became Facebook. The first time that Parker met Zuckerberg, he told him that dropping "the" in the company's name would make it more memorable.

According to the Web site TechCrunch.com, more than 85 percent of American college students used the Web site at the time, so it didn't need much help in becoming more memorable. Still, Zuckerberg had been convinced of the power of the name change. So after negotiations with a company that owned the domain name, they bought Facebook.com, becoming Facebook.

Second, Facebook opened to high school users. This was the source of much internal debate before it happened. Facebook was already known as a college Web site. Employees wondered if the site would lose some of its cool factor when it opened to high school students. Most high schools didn't offer their students personalized e-mail addresses, so it was hard to confirm that students were who they said they were. Would it be any different than MySpace? Zuckerberg was confident, though, that the move was right. He reasoned that many college students had friends who were still in high school and that users were so absorbed in what happened with their own social groups on Facebook that they didn't notice too many major changes that happened outside of their network. And for the most part, he was right. Some users protested by joining groups calling high schoolers' presence on Facebook "awkward," but before long, the protests faded away. High school students were now an accepted part of the Facebook community, and the Web site's membership climbed to five million.

PHOTOS

Another major move was adding the ability to upload photos into online albums. On Facebook, members frequently changed their profile photos. In other places on the Web, photo-hosting sites such as Flickr were becoming more popular. The Facebook team decided that there was a clear demand for college and high school students to be able to share more photographs with each other.

Facebook added a special feature called tagging to photographs. This feature allowed users to show which friends were in the photographs. Photos quickly became another way to measure social status. Just as many users tried to rack up friends, now users became obsessed with how many photos they were tagged in. This addition to the Web site was an enormous success. Facebook remains the most popular Web site for uploading photographs, even surpassing photo-hosting-only sites such as Flickr.

ADVERTISING

Of course, adding more features to Facebook meant the company was using more space on the Internet. That meant it needed even more servers in order to run well. Despite the earlier rounds of investments and the bit of advertising income that Facebook was making, it was still spending a lot of money—and it needed more.

Zuckerberg realized that he would have to get over his reluctance to include more advertisements. He preferred the groups and flyers that didn't interrupt the user's experience, but they just were not paying enough. Facebook had some luck with targeted advertising by companies such as Chase bank, which advertised its student credit card on the Web site and allowed users to share their purchase reward points with each other, and Crest White Strips, which ran a contest that rewarded a concert to the school with the most members in its Facebook group.

Microsoft, however, was ready to pay even more. Its chief competitor, Google, had recently signed a large advertising deal with MySpace, and the two companies were receiving a lot of publicity for their decision. Facebook and Microsoft both realized that their companies could benefit from a similar decision. So Microsoft committed to a large advertising deal. It would use its connections in the industry to find advertisers for Facebook. Facebook would guarantee the advertisers a certain amount of views in exchange for their payment. With this agreement, Facebook's revenue for the year doubled.

CHAPTER 4

Business Developments

In fall 2006, Mark Zuckerberg faced a new dilemma. He and his investors had agreed, through the many companies that courted them, they would have to seriously consider any offers to buy the company for $1 billion. That number may have seemed like a distant chance, but then that fall, an offer came in from technology giant Yahoo! It would pay $1 billion, but Zuckerberg was still not interested in selling. The investors and the company's board insisted that he give the offer his attention. They reminded him that it wasn't just his project he was talking about—it was an offer of a lot of money to his employees.

Zuckerberg thought what he had in the works for Facebook would increase its value even beyond $1 billion. That May, the Web site had opened to adults through networks that people could join based on where they worked. The response was not as rapid as Zuckerberg had hoped it would be—it certainly was not as instantly successful as its opening to high school students. But Zuckerberg was ready to take it a step further, and he was sure this next step would be a big one. He wanted to open Facebook to everyone in the world over the age of thirteen. His investors cited the less-than-impressive results of the work networks and doubted that opening Facebook entirely

Although Yahoo! had been one of the most popular Web sites in the earliest days of the Internet, it was struggling to define its role among tech giants in 2006. It hoped to solidify its standing by buying Facebook.

would have the wide-reaching effect he hoped for. They thought that Facebook had established itself firmly as a product for teens and young adults, and the Yahoo! offer was the best they would ever get. Tensions in the office ran high—the team was divided into the group that wanted to sell and the group that wanted to hold on.

Then Yahoo!'s stock value tumbled, and it lowered its offer to $850 million. Everyone agreed that Facebook should walk away.

THE NEWS FEED

When Facebook's other fall 2006 additions launched, some wondered if the site really had the power that Zuckerberg thought it did. All summer, programmers had been working on site features called the Mini Feed and the News Feed, which were meant to serve as resources for what was new on Facebook. The Mini Feed appeared on each person's profile, summarizing in one spot all of his or her recent activity. The News Feed collected information into a single spot where users could find the most up-to-date news on what their friends had recently updated.

Facebook turned the features on early in the morning of September 5, and the event was celebrated in the office with bottles of champagne and noisemakers. But the celebration was soon interrupted: users were instantly outraged. They said that Facebook had gone too far—it was now enabling stalking. Groups formed against the new format. Within four days, one such group had reached seven hundred thousand users. Ironically, it was the News Feed that probably allowed such fast growth to the groups—users joined as they saw on the feed that their friends had joined.

Facebook's first official reaction to this was a blog post from Zuckerberg. It was titled "Calm down. Breathe. We hear you." Some viewed this attitude as arrogant and just more proof that Zuckerberg's vision was disconnected from the reality of his program. Along with the student protest groups were scathing media reports. Soon, though, Facebook wrote new privacy codes that allowed control over what information was revealed in the feeds. Zuckerberg apologized, if not for his first blog post, for the company's lack of forethought in putting up the feeds without considering their full effect on users.

Despite the initial public relations debacle, it quickly became clear that the News Feed feature had power. Now, instead of sending information to specific friends, users were broadcasting it to everyone on their friend list. They could actively reach more people. Facebook had never really been thought of as an effective way to spread political consciousness, but now, as thousands of users daily joined the "Save Darfur" human rights group, it became evident that it had this power.

THE OPEN NETWORK

A few weeks later, the open network launched with few protests. By the end of the year, the number of users reached twelve million. Yahoo! returned, this time with an offer of more than $1 billion. But Zuckerberg had proven that the company was worth even more, and the investors agreed that he shouldn't sell.

When Facebook's networks became open to the public, users faced the question of who they should allow to have access to their profiles. Many recent and soon-to-be graduates became worried: would employers see their profiles? Since Facebook was seen as a place for social interactions, many users had made comments or posted photographs that they didn't want employers to see. Savvy users adjusted their privacy settings to make sure that only friends could access the information on their profiles. Others untagged photos and deleted comments.

Zuckerberg's take on this opening of information is not that people should censor. Instead, he believes in what he calls "radical transparency." He is quoted in *The Facebook Effect* as saying, "You have one identity." To him, it does not matter if a person is at school, at work, or with friends. That person is always the same person, no matter where he or she is. Some employers agree with this assessment—but not in a way that is favorable to users. One teacher was fired from her job after posting a picture of herself holding a mug of beer and a glass of wine. Others have been dismissed for insulting their coworkers or companies on Facebook.

For teens applying to college, the open network means a need for caution, too. A 2011 Kaplan survey says that 24 percent of surveyed admissions officers have gone to prospective students' social networking pages. To avoid being found, some users change the names on their profiles, using only a first and middle name, purposely misspelling their last name, or going by a nickname instead.

ion
people the power to
and make the world
open and connected

Mark Zuckerberg's ideas about "radical transparency" are controversial. Some people claim that by making Facebook's default settings more open to sharing information, he is deciding for them what should be public and private.

THE PLATFORM

Inspired by the success of the open network and, ultimately, of the News Feed, Facebook moved on to consider the next big thing: becoming a platform. A service or program becomes a platform when it allows other developers to create their program to be used on top of the initial service. Microsoft and Apple are both platforms for other programs. Zuckerberg wanted Facebook to provide this sort of service to become even more important to the Internet community.

Facebook solicited developers to create any sort of program they could imagine. Zuckerberg planned a special launch event called the f8 conference. He invited hundreds of developers and journalists for an announcement that he promised would change Facebook history. He unveiled his platform plans and then invited developers to participate in an event that Facebook had become legendary for: a hackathon. For eight hours, techno music blared, a lavish buffet of food was offered, and most importantly, developers wrote programming code.

The applications were an instant success. But like many other aspects of Facebook, the disconnect between Zuckerberg's hopes for the platform and its actual outcome was apparent. Some of his favorite applications were useful ones, like one that Parker cocreated to help nonprofits earn money. But the users' favorites were more often games that encouraged taking care of, or even just petting, imaginary pets. At first, Zuckerberg was opposed to interfering with production of the applications in any way. He even took down features of the Facebook site that competed directly with developers' new applications. But

Sheryl Sandberg

Sheryl Sandberg has been wildly successful in her role of chief operating officer (COO) at Facebook. She led the company to reconsider its advertisement techniques. With the input of employees, Facebook created engagement ads. These ads ask users to take an action, like commenting on a photograph or video. Of course, once a person comments, it will show up in News Feed—leading to more views. This new source of advertising has been massively successful with companies, and, according to *The Facebook Effect*, it made Facebook nearly $50 million through 2009. In addition to her financial successes, Sandberg has changed the work environment as well. Because of her, more women have been integrated into the traditionally male-dominated office. Sandberg leads conferences for female executives and encourages their growth.

the number of applications grew, and he eventually realized that the company would have to help weed them out. Finally, Facebook created a system to verify, or give a stamp of approval to, what it thought were the most useful and fun applications.

Sheryl Sandberg joined Facebook in 2008 and is seen as a major figure in turning the company into a profitable and enduring business.

THE WORLD

Facebook's next step was to open to users outside the United States. Some English-speaking countries could already access the site, but making it available to other countries would be expensive because of the necessary

servers and the work needed to make the pages translatable. Microsoft, happy with its early advertising deal that applied to ads in the United States, agreed to an advertising and investment deal that valued Facebook at $15 billion. This deal was negotiated against, once again, the backdrop of an all-night hackathon. This time, developers were working to adapt code so that it could be used in countries outside the United States.

As part of Facebook's desire to incorporate its services beyond its Web site as well as make more money, it launched a service called Beacon in early November 2007. Beacon partnered with Web sites outside of Facebook to report on users' shopping activity. When users bought an item on one of the partnering sites, an option popped up that asked them if they wanted the information broadcast to News Feed. The option popped up only for a few seconds. If users failed to select not to broadcast this information—or to opt out of the program—it would go out to all of their friends. Since it was holiday shopping season, this led to many ruined surprises. It was a disaster for Facebook because, for the first time, it had openly availed itself of users' information without explicitly getting consent. MoveOn.org, a civil action group primarily associated with political causes, led a protest. In an open letter on its Web site, it proclaimed that in this new system, "the rights of Facebook users get left behind." It demanded that "Facebook, stop invading my privacy!" Facebook took three weeks to apologize. It changed the service so that users would have to select to share information, or opt in, as opposed to selecting not to share information. This breach of trust was one of the largest in Facebook's history.

After Beacon, Facebook's board of directors encouraged Zuckerberg to find someone who could better help him manage some of the company's specifics, including its public profile and the day-to-day running of the company. Since Sean Parker's departure, Zuckerberg had filled other executive positions with several people, but none of them was a good fit for the company. But when Sheryl Sandberg, a former Google executive who had

Facebook continues to grow more and more advanced, offering new ways to communicate with other users about activities both on and off the site.

also worked as chief of staff for the U.S. Treasury Department under President Bill Clinton, joined Facebook in March 2008, a whole new world opened up. She was the first woman in such a high-level position at the company. With Sandberg in place, Zuckerberg could return to his interests, the general strategy of Facebook, and allow her to worry about the specifics of managing employees and making money.

FACEBOOK CONNECT

Just as users had calmed down after the Beacon disaster, Facebook announced yet another partnership in which Web sites shared users' information. This partnership with hundreds of Web sites is called Facebook Connect. It allows users to log in to other Web sites using their Facebook information. If, for instance, a user likes an article

Google has always been a chief competitor of Facebook, so the launch of Google's social networking site Google Plus (plus.google.com) made some Facebook executives nervous.

on a news Web site, he or she can click a button that will publish a story on his or her Facebook feed about it. Facebook viewed this not only as a way to share information with friends, but also as a means to extend its reach across the Internet. This service was not nearly as controversial as Beacon because the Facebook team had learned its lesson. They made it entirely opt in.

Still, in 2011, a blogger revealed that Facebook Connect might be reporting more information than many users realized. Even after they logged out of their accounts, five cookies—files automatically downloaded to users' computers that track Internet activity—remained active. This meant that Web sites that are a part of Facebook Connect still reported users' activity back to Facebook, although users had already signed out. Facebook said the cookies were essential to the Web site's performance. They allowed the company to track activity that prevents hackers, check the speed of the Web site's performance, and remember essential information about users' computers.

Technology bloggers acknowledged that this information could be useful to the Web site, but they still wondered why one cookie that reported back users' names to Facebook was essential. Facebook apologized and removed this particular cookie, but the four others remained. Bloggers still cautioned that, despite what Facebook says its intentions are for these cookies, they are still collecting information that users may not realize they are giving.

CHAPTER 5

Politics and Perceptions

As a political source, Facebook made its first unintentional steps with the development of the News Feed feature, which allows the rapid spread of information. In late 2007 and early 2008, Americans found themselves more politically active than ever during the presidential election year. Debates raged across the country in classrooms, offices, living rooms, and dorm rooms. As Hillary Clinton and Barack Obama gained traction in the race, people wondered, could our next president be a woman or an African American? When Arizona senator John McCain became the Republican front-runner in the race, people wondered if an older person could properly navigate the growing world of social media in a political election.

Once again, Facebook showed its ability to latch onto what people were talking about. It teamed up with ABC News to sponsor political debates just days before the

New Hampshire primary. Users made tens of thousands of comments in real time on Republican and Democrat candidates' responses. During the debate, Facebook also featured polls that allowed users to weigh in on political issues. According to the CNET News blog, more than one hundred thousand people participated. As the year wore on, more and more users chose to share their political views on Facebook by joining groups, updating statuses, or sharing relevant articles. On candidates' official pages, both supporters and opponents commented quickly and extensively. They often wrote their comments to the candidates directly, addressing them by their first names and attacking or encouraging their policies and positions. Other comments were directed at supporters or opponents, encouraging them to take action in favor of or against that candidate.

McCain struggled in the online world. He had a fraction of the fans that Obama did on his Facebook page. Both candidates completely filled out their profiles in order to seem approachable to voters; they listed their favorite books, movies, and television shows, as well as previous work experience. But while Obama's profile was updated regularly and filled with inspiring audio clips, McCain's profile lagged behind. By election time, *U.S. News and World Report* pointed out that Obama had more than two million fans on Facebook. His widespread success in the social media world was no coincidence. The person who

Through Facebook, tens of thousands of people participated in the 2008 ABC/ Facebook debate of Republican presidential candidates, marking a new shift by the company into politics.

organized his online campaign was Chris Hughes, Zuckerberg's former roommate and early Facebook spokesman. Obama's online success during the political campaign led many to wonder what it would be like to have a president who is so plugged into social media that put him into direct

contact with the people. Some predicted that social networking would bring about a whole new way of leading the country.

Obama's Facebook activity continued during his presidency. His team posted updates several times a day to his official page. The page urged people to take action for different causes by calling their congressional representatives, listed relevant information about controversial current events, celebrated victories, and, as he geared up for the 2012 election, encouraged users to donate to the campaign. Still, this consistent, online activity did not have a major effect on the way the country was run. It also didn't have much of an effect on Obama's approval ratings. As Americans faced economic hardship in 2010 and 2011, some users took to his Facebook page to demand answers, addressing the president directly as they asked why more new jobs weren't being creating and demanding the change that he had promised them. Others posted comments that celebrated small victories and told him that they were still on his side.

While some protested economic conditions on Obama's Facebook page, others took to the street—after learning about protests through Facebook. Inspired by the Arab Spring movement, the organization Adbusters

Facebook and the Arab Spring

Around the world, Facebook has proven its importance again and again as a political force. From 2010 through 2011 in Tunisia, a secretive organization named Takriz played a large part in leading a revolt against President Zine El Abidine Ben Ali. The president was accused of corruption and human rights violations. Many activists had protested him for his twenty-three years of presidency. Takriz had a Web site that was a center for this movement, and it took to other Web sites to get its message across as well. Through blogs, online forums, and finally Facebook and Twitter, protesters reached new audiences and further spread the word about government corruption and mistreatment. A particularly popular way of revealing information was through uploading videos to YouTube or to Facebook.

In July 2010, Khaled Said, a computer programmer who had videos of police officers dealing drugs, was dragged out of a cybercafé and beaten to death by the police. They claimed that he had resisted arrest. Said's family said the police feared him uploading the videos. His brother took a photograph of his dead brother and used Facebook to spread the word. What would have before been a private family's sadness became a call to action.

Thousands of users joined a group on Facebook called We Are All Khaled Said. In December, after a poor vegetable seller set himself on fire, protesters united. The weeks that followed were bloody. The police attacked protesters, and protesters took to Facebook to share their videos. The government cut off Internet access in an attempt to prevent the spread of these videos, but activists smuggled images out of the country to post them. After weeks of violence, Ben Ali finally fled Tunisia.

Countries across the Arab world have followed suit with a series of revolutions called the Arab Spring, ousting leaders, including Egyptian president Hosni Mubarak. In the article "Streetbook," an anonymous activist said, "Without the street, there's no revolution. But add Facebook to the street and you get real potential." Arizona senator John McCain, who had struggled with Facebook during the 2008 U.S. presidential election, recognized its importance here and said that Zuckerberg and his creation were the reasons why the revolutions could occur.

Other countries around the world have had their own Facebook political activism and dilemmas as well. The Web site was banned in Iran before that country's presidential elections, and China sometimes censors—and sometimes completely cuts off—access to the site.

coordinated Occupy Wall Street, a movement protesting the financial institutions that they said were to blame for the economic downturn. The group gained supporters through its Facebook page and Twitter accounts. The original plan called for protesters in New York City, but soon, parallel protests sprung up not just around the country but around the world. Most had their own Facebook page. Protesters used Facebook to document their activities, including appearances and performances from celebrity supporters and reports of arrests and accusations of police brutality. The Facebook pages also served as a way to unite supporters and provide a sense of community for a movement without one specific location or leader.

PUBLIC PERCEPTIONS

Facebook has proven itself a major player in its ability to give politicians and political causes credibility and a wide-reaching audience. In a way, it has become a news source, and users are its opinionated, although not always reliable, reporters. But for some, the question is: who really controls the information that people post to the Web site?

Many Occupy Wall Street protesters are young and Internet savvy, and social networking Web sites allow them to spread their messages around the world.

In countries like Tunisia, Egypt, China, and Iran, users expect that the government will access and attempt to censor the available information. But what about Facebook as a company—what is it doing with all of this information?

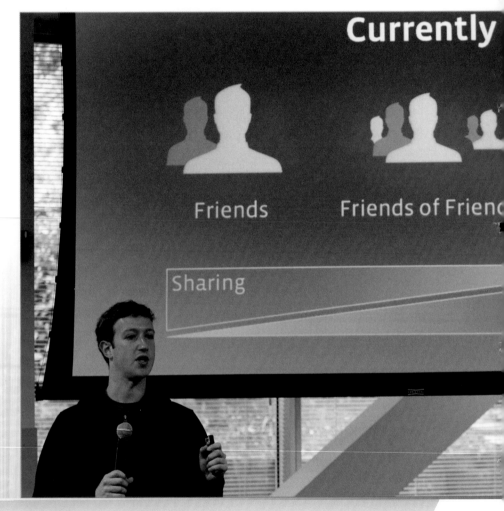

Mark Zuckerberg and other Facebook executives insist that they will never share information without your permission. However, some users and privacy groups are skeptical.

Facebook has suffered from an image problem. Despite the growing number of users, and despite—or perhaps because of—its far-reaching scope, many still don't entirely trust the service. Zuckerberg declared 2009 a serious year; he stopped wearing his famous outfit of jeans

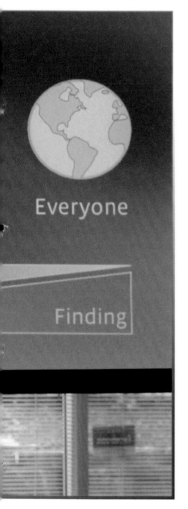

and a hooded sweatshirt and started putting on a tie each day. He was determined to show that, despite the young and cool atmosphere, the company is doing real work. Despite his newly professional image, not all Facebook users believe or trust him as a businessman. This was demonstrated once again when Facebook changed its terms-of-service agreement. The most critical perspective on this change came from the Web site the Consumerist, which noted that Facebook used to say that users' information was removed once their accounts were deactivated. The new terms of service said that the content would not expire. In a posting titled "We Can Do Anything We Want with Your Content. Forever," the Consumerist warned Facebook users to consider what they post because it won't belong to them anymore.

Mark Zuckerberg and Privacy

Although Mark Zuckerberg has repeatedly stated that he wants users to be able to control their experiences and information on Facebook, not everyone is so sure he means it. This concern was present from early on. It especially resurfaced when some of Zuckerberg's instant messages from the time right after the site's initial launch were leaked. In these messages, he said that users were stupid for trusting him with their information. He told a friend that he would give him any information he needed for the members at the time. At the same time these messages emerged, it came out that Zuckerberg used information that he had obtained from Thefacebook to hack into the e-mail of a reporter for the *Harvard Crimson* after the reporter interviewed him about the HarvardConnection controversy. Facebook confirmed that these messages and privacy breeches were true. It said, though, that these early actions were not reflective of the respectable company that it had grown into.

Although Zuckerberg's lawsuits with Eduardo Saverin and HarvardConnection had been covered in the press, they reached a new level of exposure with the 2010 premiere of the movie *The Social Network*. Based on events chronicled in Ben Mezrich's book *The Accidental Billionaires*, for which Saverin served as a major source, the movie is most often called a docudrama. It is a fictionalized account set against the backdrop of some true events. It focuses on the lawsuits from Saverin and Harvard-Connection, as well as the parties that Facebook had become so famous for.

Screenwriter Aaron Sorkin—who, ironically, was the writer for Zuckerberg's favorite show, *The West Wing*—emphasized that he wanted to tell a good story, so he wasn't concerned with accuracy. Facebook insiders who had been around during those early days said that they wished there had been as little work and as much fun and partying as the movie suggested. Still, with the story being set against the backdrop of a real company, with real characters and some inarguably real events, *The Social Network* gave critics of the site just another reason to say that Zuckerberg couldn't be trusted. That the movie was widely critically acclaimed and won three Academy Awards didn't help Facebook's cause.

Around the time that *The Social Network* premiered, Zuckerberg donated a large amount of money to public schools in Newark, New Jersey. Critics called this a calculated move to draw attention away from the negative publicity that he was receiving because of the movie. Zuckerberg insisted that it wasn't, and the recipients of the money even proclaimed that they had to convince him not to be anonymous in his donation.

Facebook defended itself by saying it was necessary legal language—it would not really use users' information without their permission. "Our philosophy that people own their information and control who they share it with has remained constant," Zuckerberg wrote on the company's blog. Facebook didn't budge on its demands, but it did reword the terms-of-service agreement so that users could better understand what they were agreeing to by using the site. After revising the wording, Facebook opened a thirty-day period during which users could comment on and vote to accept or reject the new terms of service. This was a way, Zuckerberg explained, to give them control over their Facebook experiences. If at least 30 percent of the site's active users voted, Facebook would take their decision as binding. Despite the large public outcry against the new terms-of-service agreement, Facebook did not receive the binding 30 percent required to make the vote official. Still, the majority of users who did choose to vote accepted the modified terms.

COMPETITION

Another public relations disaster for Facebook came in 2011. Google, Facebook's longtime rival, was collecting information about users' friends on Facebook and transferring that information to users' Google accounts. Facebook claimed that this was a privacy concern. It quietly hired public relations firm Burson Marsteller to spread information about Google's practices. The firm approached bloggers and other media sources to pitch the story. When it emerged that Facebook had paid the public relations company, media questioned its motives: was

When Mark Zuckerberg, seen here seated between New Jersey governor Chris Christie and Newark mayor Cory Booker, donated $100 million to Newark public schools in the midst of controversy surrounding *The Social Network*, some wondered if he was really interested in the cause or if it was just a public relations move.

Facebook really concerned about privacy? Or was it that Facebook feared this information gave Google the capability to build an equally powerful social networking site?

Google was, in fact, in the middle of launching its own social networking Web site. Called Google+, it allows users to connect with others and sort friends into relevant groups, making it easier to communicate with family, work friends, or school friends all at once, while specifying what information should be given to each group. But Facebook didn't have to worry too much about this latest competition. When Google launched its beta, or test, version of Google+, Zuckerberg signed up to check out the Web site. Within a few weeks, he became the user with the most followers.

Despite the various outrages over Facebook's actions, the company's growth did not widely suffer. Between 2008 and 2011, the Web site grew from 100 million to 750 million users. Facebook has proven itself to be a company that many users find indispensible. They may not like or trust its actions entirely. They may take to the site itself to demand changes. But they feel the need to remain connected to others by using it.

CHAPTER 6

The Future of Facebook

At the end of September 2011, during the f8 conference, Facebook announced that it was prepared to change the online world again. In the past, Facebook profiles had primarily focused on each user's day-to-day life. But what about a person's entire history? Mark Zuckerberg explained that if he is connecting with friends from years ago, he isn't interested in what they did that weekend. He wants to know where they are living and what they are doing. He wants to know what major life events have occurred since he spoke with them last. So, with that question driving the Facebook team, they launched the Timeline feature.

Timeline gives each user access to a list of every action that he or she has ever taken on Facebook. From that list, users can select important status updates, wall messages, photographs, or News Feed items to make public in their

Mark Zuckerberg

Mark Zuckerberg has been depicted in the media in a variety of ways. The leaked AIM messages from his early days with Thefacebook seem to show a person who was indifferent to his responsibility to protect the users of his product. *The Social Network* portrays him as relentless as both a partier and a businessperson, willing to step on the toes of anyone who gets in his way. Stories about his eating habits (in 2011, he decided that, to better appreciate his food, he would eat only animals that he killed himself) and his living habits (until the purchase of his home in 2011, reporters often commented on his stark and empty living space) have added to the public perception of Zuckerberg as an awkward person lacking in social skills.

But Zuckerberg's coworkers and closest friends say that these characterizations don't capture who he really is. They say that he is dedicated to his work, is a loyal friend, and is an intelligent and focused leader. They also like to remind others that Zuckerberg started the Web site when he was just nineteen years old and that he has matured since those earliest missteps. As Facebook continues to occupy a leading position in the social networking world, Zuckerberg's public persona remains a subject of popular interest.

own timelines. It's a selective digital and interactive record of each person's Facebook, and life, history. "It's the story of your life," Zuckerberg said, as reported by the *New York Times*.

In *The Facebook Effect*, technology reporter David Kirkpatrick wonders about a day when people are logged into Facebook almost without thinking about it. Similar to a computer chip that remembers information each time a computer is turned on, could Facebook one day remember all of its users' information across the Internet? As the site's platform extends, this becomes a closer possibility. But in order for it to happen, other Web sites would have to accept Facebook's role in their business, too. Not all companies are willing to take that step. They wonder if it makes sense to involve a third party in their business interactions. And what would Facebook want in return? Would it demand a share of the profits from online sales? Would it then decide what information to share with the company about its own customers?

Some people wonder if Facebook's peak has passed. After all, users consistently protest the Web site's changes. How much are users willing to take? And are there other sites that work better than Facebook? Google+ is hoping to become a replacement social network. Twitter, a Web site that allows users to broadcast brief messages to a wide audience, is gaining in popularity. And many other smaller sites might be considered more useful if a user is interested in focusing on a specific type of interaction. LinkedIn, a Web site that allows people to post their résumés and detail their work experiences, has existed since before Facebook, and it remains a major tool for connecting to the professional world. Goodreads connects people based on books that they have read or are interested in reading. As with any new feature on Facebook, Timeline stirred a wide variety of reactions. Some users protested that it, like News Feed, would make "Facebook stalking" easier. Some wondered if this would make identity theft even easier. Other users were concerned that Facebook had kept records of all their actions. Would these records always remain private? Would users always be the ones to choose which information was shared again? Facebook maintained that, yes, users will always have control over this information and what exactly is shared on their Timeline.

At the same time, Facebook also decided to step beyond Facebook Connect in its next move to expand its platform. It announced new partnerships with Web services including Netflix, Hulu, Blockbuster, and Spotify. Now, if users are watching a movie or listening to a song through one of these services, their friends can not only see a status saying that they are doing so, but also with the click of a button they can listen to the same song or watch the same movie through Facebook. It's taking online relationships beyond merely observing and commenting.

FACEBOOK USER STATISTICS

InsideFacebook.com, a popular third-party blog that follows Facebook news as well as usage statistics, provoked media frenzy in June 2011 when it announced that Facebook had lost six million users in the United States in the previous month. Some predicted that this was the beginning of the end for the social networking Web site. But in a follow-up post, the blog explained that there is no single reliable way for sources outside of the company to effectively track users' time and activity on the site. Facebook claims that the information InsideFacebook.com had been using, which is a general estimate provided to potential advertisers, is not a reliable source for such specifics. The blog also noted inconsistencies in other third-party groups' reporting of traffic for previous months. Some claimed that the Web site grew or remained steady, while others claimed that it declined. Facebook's official statement was that it was happy with the rate at which it continued to grow.

CRITICISMS

A major critique of Facebook is that it has grown too big. It no longer specializes in just connecting people. Now

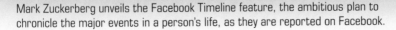

Mark Zuckerberg unveils the Facebook Timeline feature, the ambitious plan to chronicle the major events in a person's life, as they are reported on Facebook.

people are interacting not just with each other, but also with a variety of applications and information posted by outsiders. One of Zuckerberg's criticisms of houseSYSTEM, the early social networking Web site created by a Harvard student, was that the program offered too many options for its users. As Facebook expands its partnerships with media companies and adds interactions that seek to define an entire life, critics wonder if Facebook could fall victim to this same problem. Has it finally gone too far?

As users routinely protest program updates, some would say yes. But the numbers tell a different story. Countries whose citizens have long been active on the site, such as the United States and Canada, have not seen as much rapid growth in membership as they did during the site's early years. This is simply because so many people already have profiles on the site. And despite current users' protests, Facebook has not seen a major drop in usage.

People may be threatening to leave Facebook, but when so many have already established an expanded social life through their profile, it's hard to transfer that to a different social network—or to disconnect entirely.

Even if the end of Facebook's reign as the king of social media arrives, its time on top has had an immeasurable impact on individuals and on society as a whole. From the

Facebook's, and hence Mark Zuckerberg's, popularity is unprecedented and show no signs of retreating.

families and friends reunited to countries starting revolutions, Facebook has changed the way that people share information and communicate with others.

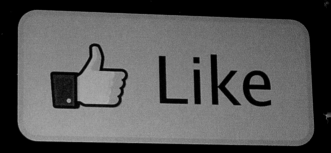

For billions of people around the world, Facebook has become a part of everyday life, and the "Like" button has become a symbol of the world's fascination with the social network.

FUTURE POSSIBILITIES

In January 2011, Facebook raised $11.5 billion to continue its operations. In doing so, it added more shareholders, taking the number to more than five hundred. Federal laws state that when a company has more than five hundred shareholders, it must go public or disclose its financial records. Going public means that the previously private shares that were only Facebook's to give will be available for purchase by the general public. In 2012, it finally announced plans to do so. On February 1, Facebook officially filed for a $5 Billion Initial Public Offering (IPO), putting it on track to be the largest ever for an Internet company. Based on the amount of stock offered estimates would value the 8-year-old business at nearly $100 billion, much higher than many longer-established American companies. Mark Zuckerberg's personal 28.2 percent ownership would make his personal net worth more than $28 billion, establishing him as one of the world's richest people.

MARK ZUCKERBERG AND FACEBOOK

MARK ZUCKERBERG

Full name: Mark Zuckerberg

Birth date: May 14, 1984

Birthplace: Dobbs Ferry, New York

Current residence: Palo Alto, California

College attended: Harvard University, two years completed

Current job: Founder and CEO of Facebook

Net worth: $17.7 billion (Pre-IPO)

Marital status: Dating longtime partner Priscilla Chan

Most popular outfit: T-shirt, jeans, and Adidas flip-flop sandals

FACEBOOK

Founders: Mark Zuckerberg, Eduardo Saverin, Dustin Moskovitz, and Chris Hughes

Board of directors: Mark Zuckerberg, Marc Andreessen, Jim Breyer, Don Graham, Reed Hastings, Erskine Bowles, and Peter Thiel

Date it went live: February 4, 2004

Annual revenue: $4.27 billion

Net worth: Estimated $80–$100 billion

Number of users: 800 million

Number of employees: 2,000+

National headquarters: Palo Alto, California

Average number of friends per user: 130

Average number of photos uploaded per day: 250 million

Average number of posts commented on or liked per day: 2 billion

Percent of users who log in at least once a day: Over 50 percent

Timeline

October 2003 Mark Zuckerberg creates Facemash, a program for Harvard students seen as a predecessor to Facebook.

February 2004 Zuckerberg launches a social networking service at Harvard called Thefacebook.

March 2004 Thefacebook expands beyond Harvard to other Ivy League schools.

May 2004 Thefacebook spreads to colleges beyond the Ivy Leagues.

June 2004 Thefacebook moves to Palo Alto, California; Sean Parker joins the team.

July 2004 Thefacebook incorporates as a company.

September 2004 Thefacebook receives its first investment of $600,000 from Peter Thiel and other smaller investors.

November 2004 Thefacebook reaches one million users.

April 2005 Thefacebook raises $12.7 million in funding from Accel Partners and other smaller investors.

September 2005 Thefacebook opens to high school students and changes its name to Facebook.

October 2005 The photo application is added to Facebook; it remains one of the most popular features on the Web site.

May 2006 Facebook opens to work networks.

Summer 2006 Yahoo! makes a $1 billion offer to buy Facebook.

September 2006 Facebook adds the News Feed and Mini Feed features, to the dismay of many users. In response, Facebook quickly revamps the privacy settings to allow users more control over what information they share. Facebook opens to users worldwide age thirteen and older.

May 2007 Facebook launches its Facebook platform, allowing outside developers to create programs to be run on the Web site.

November 2007 Facebook launches Beacon, the short-lived advertising tool that reported users' activities from other Web sites back to users' news feeds.

April 2008 Facebook releases Facebook Chat. It settles its lawsuit with the Winklevoss twins for a settlement estimated at $65 million.

August 2008 Facebook reaches over one hundred million users.

January 2009 Zuckerberg declares 2009 a serious year and decides to wear a tie to work.

February 2009 Facebook modifies its terms-of-service agreement, leading to protests from many users and bloggers. In response, Facebook holds an open vote for users to decide if the modified terms of service are fair.

June 2010–March 2011 A series of uprisings in the Arab world, known as the Arab Spring, lead to overthrows of several political leaders. Facebook is credited with being a major part of the movement because it provided a central location for activists to coordinate protests and spread information.

October 2010 The movie *The Social Network* is released.

May 2011 The ConnectU team's appeal is denied—the original settlement from 2008 stands.

July 2011 Facebook reaches 750 million active users.

September 2011 Facebook announces its Timeline feature, which aims to provide a comprehensive overview of the important events in a user's life, as shown on a public timeline.

Glossary

code The language in which computer programs and Web sites are written.

cookie A file automatically downloaded to a computer that tracks a user's actions.

cyberbullying The use of technology, including social media Web sites, to threaten or harass another person.

developer A person who creates computer programs or code for Web sites.

engagement advertisement An ad that asks users to participate by leaving a comment or taking an action on Facebook.

News Feed Information about friends' recent Facebook activity, consolidated on one Web page.

opt-in A service that users explicitly select to use.

opt-out A service that users automatically are entered into use of unless they select not to.

platform A system that provides the underlying structure that allows other programs to run. Windows and Apple are examples of different platforms.

profile A central place for information about a user, including school, location, and interests.

server A physical computer that executes commands associated with a specific program. Generally, servers are better able to handle large amounts of traffic and data requests than an average computer.

share A small percentage of ownership in a company.

social network Any Web site such as Facebook, MySpace, Twitter, or LinkedIn that allows users to interact with each other in an online community.

tagging Linking a photograph or note directly to a user to indicate that user's connection to the post.

venture capitalist A person or company that provides early funding as an investment in a company before it is established enough to obtain bank loans. Venture capitalists often gain shares and a varying amount of control over the company's operations to ensure that they will make back the money that they invested.

wall A Facebook feature that allows users to post public comments to each other's profiles.

For More Information

Canadian Centre for Child Protection
615 Academy Road
Winnipeg, MB R3N 0E7
Canada
(800) 532-9135
Web site: http://www.protectchildren.ca
The Canadian Centre for Child Protection is a nonprofit
organization that registers abuse reports, raises public
awareness of safety tips, and works to prevent abuse.

Center for Internet Security
31 Tech Valley Drive
East Greenbush, NY 12061
(518) 266-3460
Web site: http://www.cisecurity.org
The Center for Internet Security is a nonprofit organization focused on identifying and advocating for online
security standards.

Center for Technology and National Security Policy
National Defense University

300 5th Avenue SW

Fort Lesley J. McNair

Washington, DC 20319

(202) 685-2529

Web site: http://www.ndu.edu/CTNSP

The Center for Technology and National Security Policy is
a think tank that studies a number of topics, including
technology and social networking, in order to better
educate politicians.

CyberSmart Curriculum

650 Townsend, Suite 435

San Francisco, CA 94103

(415) 863-0600

Web site: http://www.cybersmartcurriculum.org

CyberSmart Curriculum is an organization that provides
Internet safety information that is easily incorporated
into classroom curriculums.

Electronic Privacy Information Center

1718 Connecticut Avenue NW, Suite 200

Washington, DC 20009

(202) 483-1140

Web site: http://www.epic.org

The Electronic Privacy Center is a research firm dedicated to
examining civil liberty issues that relate to the Internet.

Future Business Leaders of America
1912 Association Drive
Reston, VA 20191-1591
(800) 325-2946
Web site: http://www.fbla-pbl.org
This national organization teaches middle and high school
students the skills they need to succeed in business careers.

The Information Technology & Innovation Foundation
1101 K Street NW, #610
Washington, DC 20005
(202) 449-1351
Web site: http://www.itif.org
The Information Technology & Innovation Foundation is
a nonprofit think tank promoting public policy information related to computer and technology issues.

Junior Achievement
One Education Way
Colorado Springs, CO 80906
(719) 540-8000
Web site: http://www.ja.org
Junior Achievement is an organization that teaches teens
skills essential to succeed in the business world.

Pew Internet & American Life Project
1615 L Street, NW, Suite 700

Washington, DC 20036

(202) 419-4500

Web site: http://www.pewinternet.org

The Pew Internet & American Life Project is a project from the Pew Research Center, a nonprofit think tank. The project aims to examine how advances in the Internet and technology change daily life for average citizens.

Web Aware

50 Gladstone Avenue, Suite 120

Ottawa, ON K1Y 3E6

Canada

(613) 224-7721

Web site: http://www.bewebaware.ca

Web Aware is an Internet safety–focused segment of Media Awareness Network, a major nonprofit organization that distributes information on digital literacy to teens, parents, and educators.

WEB SITES

Due to the changing nature of Internet links, Rosen Publishing has developed an online list of Web sites related to the subject of this book. This site is updated regularly. Please use this link to access the list:

http://www.rosenlinks.com/ibio/zuck

For Further Reading

Anderson, M.T. *Feed*. New York, NY: HarperCollins, 2005.

Asher, Jay, and Carolyn Mackler. *The Future of Us*. New York, NY: Razorbill, 2011.

Catfish. DVD. 83 minutes. Directed by Henry Joost and Ariel Shulman. Universal Pictures, 2010.

Cleveland, Donald. *Seven Wonders of Communication*. Minneapolis, MN: Lerner Books, 2010.

Cook, Collen Ryckert. *Frequently Asked Questions About Social Networking*. New York, NY: Rosen Publishing, 2011.

Kowalski, Robin C., Susan P. Limber, and Patricia W. Agatson. *Cyber Bullying: Bullying in the Digital Age*. Hoboken, NJ: Wiley, 2007.

Lohr, Steve. *Digital Revolutionaries: The Men and Women Who Brought Computing to Life*. New York, NY: Flash Point, 2009.

Lüsted, Marcia Amidon. *Social Networking: MySpace, Facebook, and Twitter* (Technology Pioneers). Edina, MN: ABDO Publishing, 2011.

Maida, Jerome, and Fritz Saalfield. *Mark Zuckerberg: Creator of Facebook*. Vancouver, WA: Bluewater Productions: 2011.

Mezrich, Ben. *The Founding of Facebook, a Tale of Sex, Money, Genius, and Betrayal.* New York, NY: Doubleday, 2009.

Mooney, Carla. *Online Social Networking.* New York, NY: Gale Cengage Learning, 2009.

Ryan, Peter K. *Social Networking.* New York, NY: Rosen Publishing, 2011.

Shih, Clara. *The Facebook Era: Tapping Online Social Networks to Build Better Products, Reach New Audiences, and Sell More Stuff.* Upper Saddle River, NJ: Prentice Hall, 2009.

The Social Network. DVD. 120 minutes. Directed by David Fincher. Columbia Pictures, 2010.

Solow, Jennifer. *The Aristobrats.* New York, NY: Sourcebooks, 2010.

Stewart, Gail B. *Mark Zuckerberg: Facebook Creator.* Farmington Hills, MI: KidHaven, 2009.

Whiting, Jim. *Online Communication and Social Networking.* San Diego, CA: Referencepoint Press, 2011.

Bibliography

Auletta, Ken. "A Woman's Place." *New Yorker*, July 11, 2011. Retrieved July 2011 (http://www.newyorker.com/reporting/2011/07/11/110711fa_fact_auletta).

Broache, Anne. "Information Overload in the Facebook Presidential Debates?" CNET, January 6, 2008. Retrieved January 2011(http://news.cnet.com/8301-10784_3-9841291-7.html).

de la Merced, Michael J. "Facebook Completes $1.5 Billion Raising Round." *New York Times*, January 21, 2011. Retrieved July 2011(http://dealbook.nytimes.com/2011/01/21/facebook-completes-1-5-billion-fundraising-round).

Facebook. "Factsheet." 2011. Retrieved September 2011 (https://www.facebook.com/press/info.php?factsheet).

Hoffan, Jan. "As Bullies Go Digital, Parents Play Catch-up." *New York Times*, December 4, 2010. Retrieved July 2011. (http://www.nytimes.com/2010/12/05/us/05bully.html).

Kaplan.com. "Facebook Checking Is No Longer Unchartered Territory in College Admissions." September 22, 2011. Retrieved September 2011(http://www.kaplan.com/aboutkaplan/newsroom/Pages/newsroom.aspx?ID=639).

Kirkpatrick, David. *The Facebook Effect*. New York, NY: Simon & Schuster, 2010.

Lacy, Sarah. *Once You're Lucky, Twice You're Good: The Rebirth of Silicon Valley and the Rise of Web 2.0*. New York, NY: Penguin Books, 2008.

MoveOn.org. "MoveOn.org Civic Action: Facebook Must Respect Privacy." November 20, 2007. Retrieved September 2011 (http://civ.moveon.org/facebookprivacy/071120email.html).

Pollock, John. "Streetbook." *Technology Review*, October 20, 2011. Retrieved October 2011 (http://www.technologyreview.com/web/38379).

Sengupta, Somini, and Ben Sisario. "Facebook as Tastemaker." *New York Times*, September 22, 2011. Retrieved September 2011 (http://www.nytimes.com/2011/09/23/technology/facebook-makes-a-push-to-be-a-media-hub.html?).

Walters, Chris. "Facebook's New Terms of Service: 'We Can Do Anything We Want with Your Content. Forever.'" *Consumerist*, February 15, 2009. Retrieved September 2011(http://consumerist.com/2009/02/facebooks-new-terms-of-service-we-can-do-anything-we-want-with-your-content-forever.html).

Zuckerberg, Mark. "On Facebook, People Own and Control Their Information." Facebook Blog, February 16, 2009. Retrieved September 2011(http://www.facebook.com/blog.php?post=54434097130).

Index

ABOUT THE AUTHOR

Susan Dobinick lives in New York City and works in youth media. She has had a Facebook account for more than six years.

PHOTO CREDITS

Cover, pp. 3, 6–7, 48–49, 51, 74–75 Bloomberg via Getty Images; p. 14 Photo by Erik Klein, webmaster@vintage-computer.com; pp. 16–17 56–57, 58–59, 60–61, 70–71, 76–77, 93 © AP Images; pp. 19, 20–21 Rick Friedman; p. 25 Merrick Morton/© Columbia Pictures/Courtesy Everett Collection; pp. 26–27 © Nomad/SuperStock; pp. 28, 66–67, 100–101, 102–103, 104–105 Justin Sullivan/Getty Images; p. 32 Washington Post/Getty Images; p. 35 Jason Kempin/Getty Images; p. 41 Alex Wong/Getty Images; p. 42 Spencer Platt/Getty Images; pp. 46–47 Chip Somodevilla/Getty Images; p. 78 © www.istockphoto.com/Andrea Zanchi; pp. 82–83, 86–87 Emmanuel Dunand/AFP/Getty Images; pp. 88–89 Kimberly White/Getty Images; chapter openers, interior graphics Shutterstock.com.

Designer: Nicole Russo; Editor: Nicolas Croce;
Photo Researcher: Marty Levick